GRANDMA SANKOFA'S HOUSE

Love + Listen

GRANDMA SANKOFA'S HOUSE

Copyright © 2020 by Dr. Talaya L. Tolefree

Written by Dr. Talaya L. Tolefree

Illustrated by Joyeeta Neogi

All rights reserved. No part of this book may be used or reproduced in any manner whatsoever without the prior written permission of the author.

BOOK DEDICATION

I dedicate this book to my daughter Nia-Imani, my late granny Estelle Kennedy, my mentor Rev. Dr. Paulette E. Sankofa and to generations of powerful women and girls of African descent all over the world who have nurtured the lives of so many by developing strong relationships.

Continue to be your Sistah Queen's keeper!

"Hi Savannah! I'm glad you get to go to Grandma Sankofa's with me again!"

"Nia, I can't wait to go...we always have such fun, what happened the last time you went to Grandma Sankofa's?" asked Savannah.

"Tag...you're it! If you push me on the swing, I will tell you the whole story," said Nia.

"Ok...but you have to promise not to jump off the swing like you did the last time," Savannah giggled.

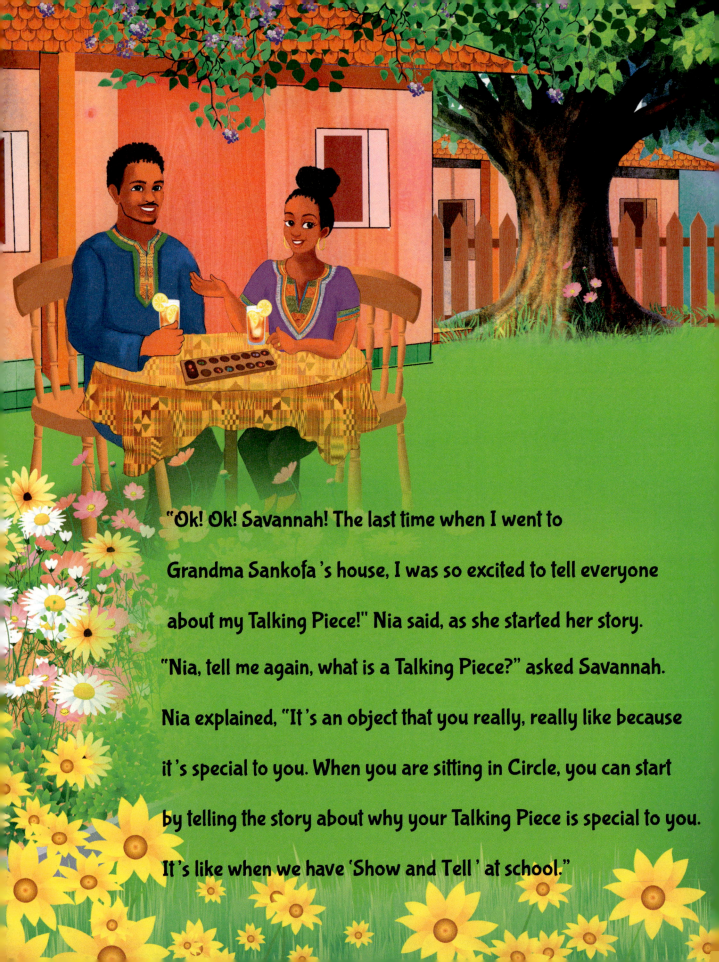

"Ok! Ok! Savannah! The last time when I went to Grandma Sankofa's house, I was so excited to tell everyone about my Talking Piece!" Nia said, as she started her story.

"Nia, tell me again, what is a Talking Piece?" asked Savannah.

Nia explained, "It's an object that you really, really like because it's special to you. When you are sitting in Circle, you can start by telling the story about why your Talking Piece is special to you. It's like when we have 'Show and Tell' at school."

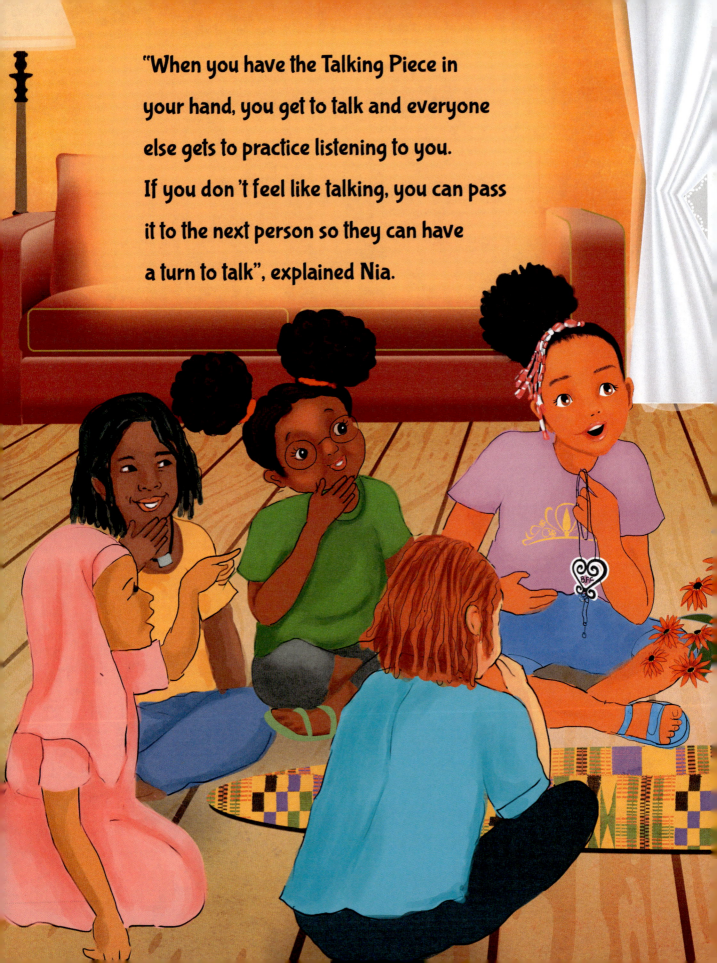

"When you have the Talking Piece in your hand, you get to talk and everyone else gets to practice listening to you. If you don't feel like talking, you can pass it to the next person so they can have a turn to talk", explained Nia.

"Ok, so everyone gets a turn to talk and a turn to listen?" asked Savannah.

"Yep, that's right Savannah and everyone has such exciting stories to tell! I love listening to my friends share about what's important to them. Now it's your turn to listen while I finish telling you the story about Grandma Sankofa's house," Nia continued.

Grandma Sankofa greeted me and my parents at the door. "Good Morning, Grandma Sankofa! I brought a Talking Piece for our Circle today!" Nia announced.

"Great, Nia! You can tell your friends all about your Talking Piece after the welcoming and opening for our Circle," said Grandma Sankofa.

"Well, good morning everyone! It's time for our morning Circle. Grandma Sankofa is so proud to have you all here this morning. Now that you have finished your breakfast, let's do a quick body check to make sure we are ready for our Circle," said Grandma Sankofa. as she welcomed the children and prepared to start the Circle.

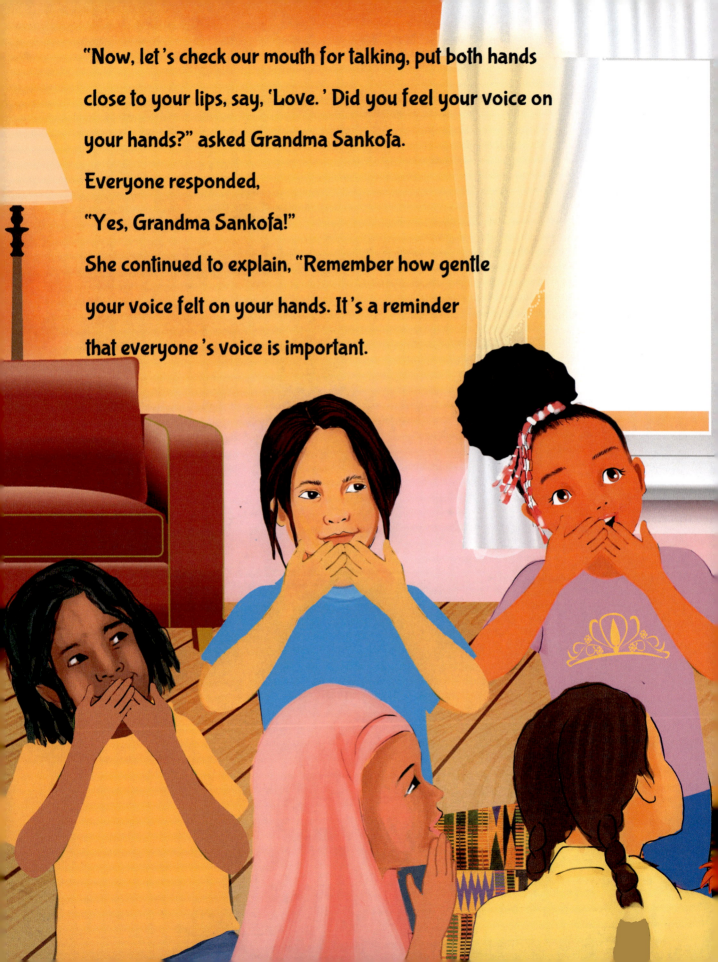

"Now, let's check our mouth for talking, put both hands close to your lips, say, 'Love.' Did you feel your voice on your hands?" asked Grandma Sankofa.

Everyone responded,

"Yes, Grandma Sankofa!"

She continued to explain, "Remember how gentle your voice felt on your hands. It's a reminder that everyone's voice is important.

We have to listen carefully to everyone's words and we have to be gentle with their words. We don't share them unless we have permission, right?"

The children answered, "Right Grandma Sankofa!"

Grandma Sankofa softly said,

"Now be still and quiet. Let's check our ears for listening.

Gently pull on your left ear... and now your right ear.

Can you hear the silence in the room?"

"Yes, Grandma Sankofa!" the children responded.

"Good job! Sitting still and being quiet is

one way we can relax our bodies and focus,"

Grandma Sankofa said as the Circle began.

Grandma Sankofa continued,
"Now let's check our eyes for connecting. Everybody look at the beautiful flowers in the center of our Circle. I picked them from our garden. Now, turn to each one of your friends and look them in their eyes. Do we all feel connected?"
"Yes, Grandma Sankofa!" the children responded as they made connections with their eyes.

"Remember, last week we listened to the sounds from African drums and we learned that long ago African drummers used drumming to talk to their community? That drumming sound is like the sound we hear from our heartbeat. Now, let's put our hand over our chest and feel our heartbeat. It sounds like the beats from African drummers," said Grandma Sankofa.

Does everybody feel their heartbeat?"

"Yes, Grandma Sankofa!

"Our heart is for loving and feeling. Our heartbeat reminds us that we are all human beings."

all the children responded.

Our heartbeat reminds us that we are all human beings.

Grandma Sankofa wrote our opening message on her whiteboard, "Love is the Key to everything!" "Now, let's read it together along with this week's values," said Grandma Sankofa.

Love is the Key to everything

Love is the Key to everything.

Everyone responded,

"Love is the Key to everything!

Our values are, Love and Listen."

Grandma Sankofa said, "Yes! You got it!

Let's remember our values as we continue

with our Circle."

Our values are, Love and Listen.

Grandma Sankofa smiles and says, "Nia, it's time for you to share the story about your Talking Piece with us."

"My Talking Piece is a necklace with a heart shaped charm. It says 'BFF.' My necklace is special to me because my best friend forever, Savannah, gave it to me. Savannah and I have been best friends since we were two years old. We both love to cook and play outside!" said Nia.

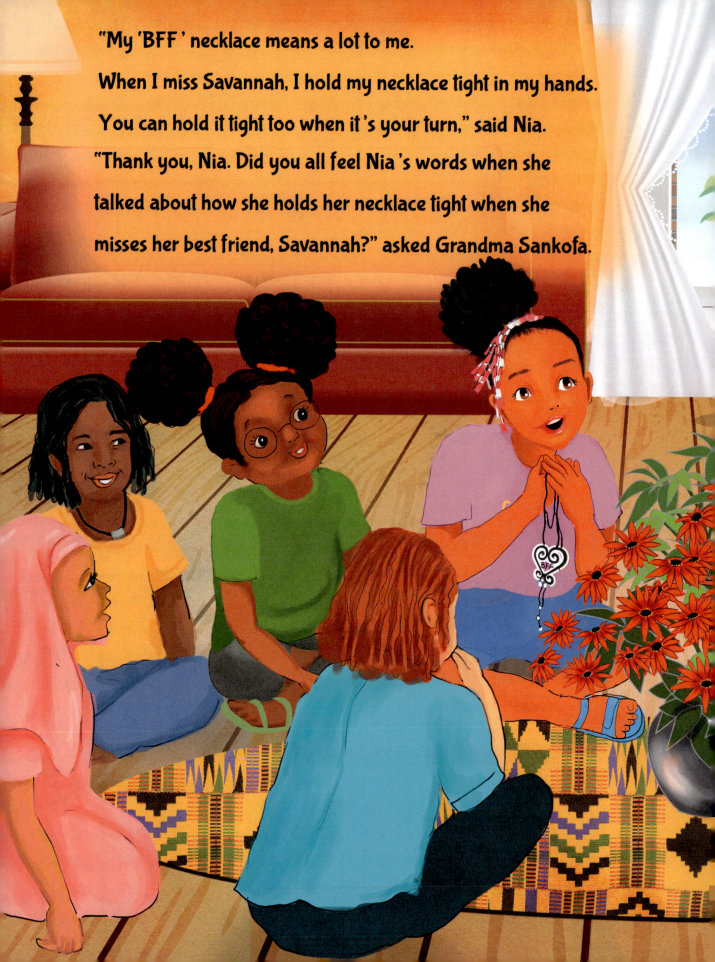

"My 'BFF' necklace means a lot to me. When I miss Savannah, I hold my necklace tight in my hands. You can hold it tight too when it's your turn," said Nia.

"Thank you, Nia. Did you all feel Nia's words when she talked about how she holds her necklace tight when she misses her best friend, Savannah?" asked Grandma Sankofa.

"Our question for the day is, 'What made you smile today?' said Heaven. "All the children got a turn to hold my Talking Piece and share about what made them smile. They answered with such joy and excitement!" said Nia.

Grandma Sankofa closed by saying,

"Please turn to your friend and repeat this rhyme

'Be a good friend, love and listen until the end!'

Well, that ends our Circle, friends.

Thank you for joining us, see you at our next Circle."

Be a good friend, love and listen until the end!

"Wow Nia! That was a great story!" said Savannah.

"Thank you...I want to be a storyteller just like Grandma Sankofa when I grow up." said Nia.

"Me too, we can tell stories about how to be good friends, love and listen until the end!" said Savannah.

"Yes! You got it!" said Nia.

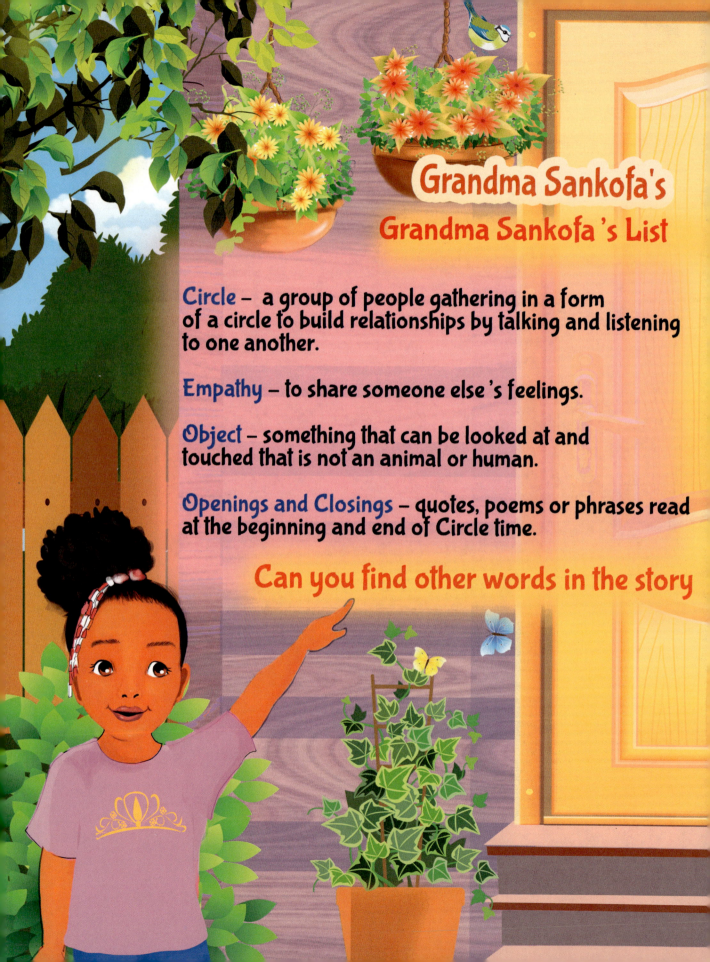

Grandma Sankofa's List

Circle – a group of people gathering in a form of a circle to build relationships by talking and listening to one another.

Empathy – to share someone else's feelings.

Object – something that can be looked at and touched that is not an animal or human.

Openings and Closings – quotes, poems or phrases read at the beginning and end of Circle time.

Can you find other words in the story

House
of Words to Practice

Relax – to calm your body and thoughts; to be still and comfortable.

Responded – to give your answer to a question or action.

Talking Piece – an object that has special meaning. The person with the Talking Piece gets to talk and everyone else practices listening.

Value – a belief about what is right and important.

that you would like to practice?

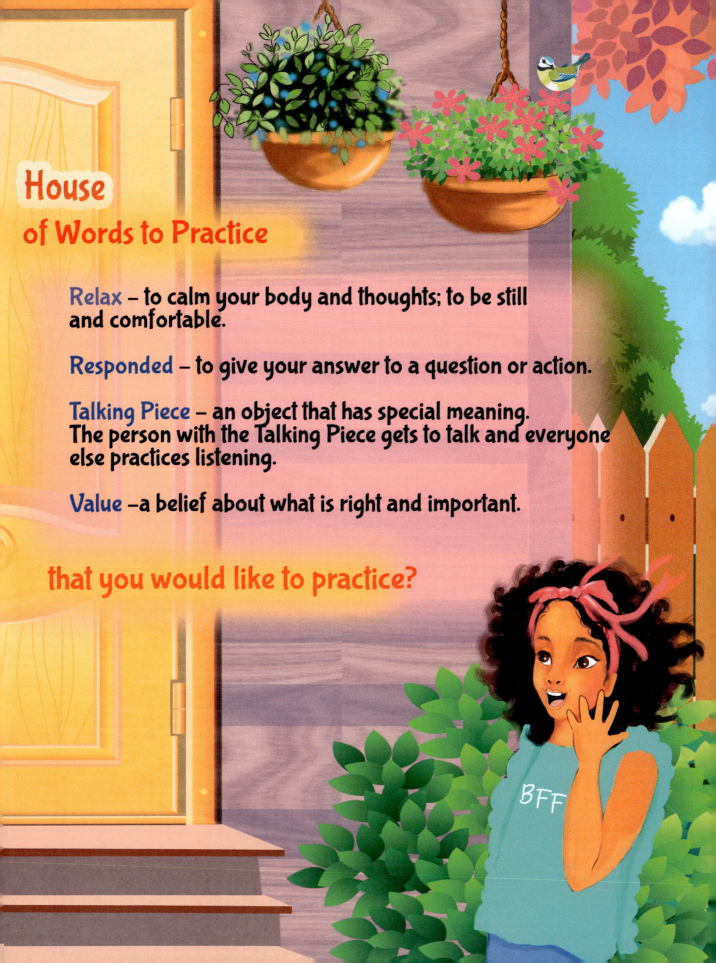

The Sankofa Circle ©

The Sankofa Circle is one that goes round and round, it has a beginning but never ends.

The Sankofa Circle guides us to look back into our past to bring forth knowledge and wisdom into our present. The knowledge and wisdom from our past are full of lived experiences that characterize the complexities of our humanity.

The Sankofa Circle helps us to be self-determined and dare to think for ourselves as we birth our future. It compels us to Love and Listen to wisdom as she calls, lives and breathes through our ancestors, elders, children, through us…through our community.

The Sankofa Circle gives us courage to see our failures and shortcomings as opportunities for growth. We celebrate our successes and those who helped us along the way.

Voices that have been unheard are now heard and those who have been treated as invisible are now visible.

The Sankofa Circle is a healing process of building human relationships through lived experiences, it goes round and round, it has a beginning but never ends – Sankofa.

~Dr. Talaya L. Tolefree

Copyright © 2020 All Rights Reserved

Made in the USA
Monee, IL
11 July 2021